God's Little Instruction Book for New Believers

P. O. Box 55388
Tulsa, Oklahoma

2nd Printing
Over 18,000 in Print

God's Little Instruction Book for New Believers
ISBN 1-56292-101-0
Copyright ©1996 by Honor Books, Inc.
P. O. Box 55388
Tulsa, Oklahoma 75155

Printed in the United States of America. All rights reserved under International Copyright Law. Contents and/or cover may not be reproduced in whole or in part in any form without the express written consent of the Publisher.

God's Little Instruction Book for New Believers

Welcome to God's family!

Affirmation of Faith

I have received Jesus Christ as my personal Lord and Savior. I believe He died on the cross for my sins and God resurrected Him from the dead to give me a new life. He loved me so much that He gave His life for me, and now I have given my life to Him.

Signed:______________________________

Therefore if any man be in Christ,
he is a new creature:
old things are passed away;
behold, all things are become new.

2 Corinthians 5:17

Let us then approach the throne of grace with confidence, so that we may receive mercy and find grace to help us in our time of need.
Hebrews 4:16 NIV

The greatest privilege God gives to you is the freedom to approach Him at any time.

Do not face a day until you have faced God.

O God...early will I seek thee: my soul thirsteth for thee, my flesh longeth for thee in a dry and thirsty land, where no water is.
Psalm 63:1

Give, and it will be given to you. A good measure, pressed down, shaken together and running over, will be poured into your lap. For with the measure you use, it will be measured to you.
Luke 6:38 NIV

Love is the one business in which it pays to be an absolute spendthrift: give it away; throw it away; splash it over; empty your pockets; shake the basket; and tomorrow you'll have more than ever.

You can give without loving, but you cannot love without giving.

Excel in this grace of giving. I am not commanding you, but I want to test the sincerity of your love.
2 Corinthians 8:7-8 NIV

All scripture is given by inspiration of God, and is profitable for doctrine, for reproof, for correction, for instruction in righteousness.
2 Timothy 3:16

The Bible is the special, very own Book, Writing, and Word of the Holy Spirit.

Whenever a man reads the Word of God, the Holy Spirit is speaking to him.

No prophecy of scripture is of any private interpretation, for prophecy never came by the will of man, but holy men of God spoke as they were moved by the Holy Spirit.
2 Peter 1:20-21
NKJV

And the peace of God, which passeth all understanding, shall keep your hearts and minds through Christ Jesus.
Philippians 4:7

Being at peace with yourself is a direct result of finding peace with God.

A great many people are trying to make peace, but that has already been done. God has not left it for us to do; all we have to do—is to enter into it.

Thou wilt keep him in perfect peace, whose mind is stayed on thee: because he trusteth in thee.
Isaiah 26:3

Like newborn babies, crave pure spiritual milk, so that by it you may grow up in your salvation, now that you have tasted that the Lord is good.
1 Peter 2:2-3 NIV

And as a new-born babe he gladly receives the *sincere milk of the Word, and grows thereby*...from faith to faith, from grace to grace, until at length he comes into *a perfect man, unto the measure of the stature of the fullness of Christ.*

From the time of our being "born again" the gradual work of sanctification takes place. We are enabled *by the Spirit* to *mortify the deeds of the body*, of our evil nature, and as we are more and more dead to sin, we are more and more alive to God.

For if you live according to the sinful nature, you will die; but if by the Spirit you put to death the misdeeds of the body, you will live, because those who are led by the Spirit of God are the sons of God.
Romans 8:13-14
NIV

Let us not give up meeting together, as some are in the habit of doing, but let us encourage one another.
Hebrews 10:25 NIV

The difference between listening to a radio sermon and going to church...is almost like the difference between calling your girl on the phone and spending an evening with her.

Church attendance is as vital to a disciple as a transfusion of rich, healthy blood to a sick man.

If you abide in My word, you are My disciples indeed. And you shall know the truth, and the truth shall make you free.
John 8:31-32
NKJV

Grace and peace be multiplied unto you through the knowledge of God, and of Jesus our Lord, According as his divine power hath given unto us all things that pertain unto life and godliness, through the knowledge of him that hath called us to glory and virtue.

2 Peter 1:2-3

Success is...seeking, knowing, loving and obeying God. If you seek, you will know; if you know, you will love; if you love, you will obey.

He that has learned to obey will know how to command.

The wise in heart
accept commands,
but a chattering
fool comes
to ruin.
Proverbs 10:8 NIV

Casting all your anxiety upon Him, because He cares for you.
1 Peter 5:7 NASB

Give your troubles to God; He will be up all night anyway.

Prayer can change what arguments can't settle.

Love your enemies, bless them that curse you, do good to them that hate you, and pray for them which despitefully use you, and persecute you.
Matthew 5:44

If we confess our sins, He is faithful and just to forgive us our sins and to cleanse us from all unrighteousness.
1 John 1:9 NKJV

Father, accept my imperfect repentance, be compassionate toward my infirmities, purify my uncleanness, strengthen my weakness, fix my unstableness, and let thy good Spirit watch over me forever, and thy love ever rule in my heart. Amen.

To believers in Christ who walk in this way, there is no condemnation for their past sins. God does not condemn their past. It is as though these past sins had never been, as if a stone were thrown to the bottom of the sea.

As far as the east
is from the west,
so far has He
removed our
transgressions
from us.
Psalm 103:12
NASB

Trust in the Lord with all your heart and lean not on your own understanding.
Proverbs 3:5 NIV

Give me a task too big, too hard for human hands, then I shall come at length to lean on thee, and leaning, find my strength.

If God be your partner, make your plans large.

I can do all things through Christ which strengtheneth me.
Philippians 4:13

So work with fear and trembling to discover what it really means to be saved. God is working in you to make you willing and able to obey him.
Philippians 2:12-13 CEV

Old patterns will persist if serious effort is not made to change them.

You are what you think about.

Lead every thought and purpose away captive into the obedience of Christ.
2 Corinthians 10:5 AMP

Your face, Lord,
do I seek.
Psalm 27:8 NRSV

To pray does not only mean to seek help; it also means to seek Him.

No prayer of adoration will ever soar higher than a simple cry: "I love You, God."

And though you have not seen Him, you love Him, and though you do not see Him now, but believe in Him, you greatly rejoice with joy inexpressible and full of glory.
1 Peter 1:8 NASB

Be therefore imitators of God as His beloved children, and live in love, as Christ also loved us and gave Himself for us.
Ephesians 5:1-2
MLB

Imitating Christ is opening the door to friendship.

A faithful friend is an image of God.

But we all, as with unveiled face we see as in a mirror the Lord's glory reflected, are changed into the same likeness from one degree of glory to another.
2 Corinthians 3:18 MLB

For God so loved the world, that he gave his only begotten Son, that whosoever believeth in him should not perish, but have everlasting life.
John 3:16

There is no father on earth who has as much love in his heart as God has for you. You may be sinful as hell; yet God stands ready and willing to receive you to His bosom and to forgive you freely.

[Rely] simply on Him that loves you, and whom you love; just as a little helpless child. Christ is yours, all yours: that is enough. Lean your whole soul upon Him!

Trust in the Lord with all thine heart; and lean not unto thine own understanding.
Proverbs 3:5

If you are willing and obedient, you will eat the best from the land.
Isaiah 1:19 NIV

Depend on it, God's work done in God's way will never lack God's supplies.

I am only one; but still I am one. I cannot do everything, but still I can do something; I will not refuse to do the something I can do.

Under his (Christ's) direction the whole body is fitted together perfectly, and each part in its own special way helps the other parts.
Ephesians 4:16
TLB

He who heeds discipline shows the way to life, but whoever ignores correction leads others astray.
Proverbs 10:17 NIV

An error doesn't become a mistake until you refuse to correct it.

When you make a mistake, admit it; learn from it and don't repeat it.

Godly sorrow brings repentance that leads to salvation and leaves no regret.
2 Corinthians 7:10 NIV

Then you will call upon me and come and pray to me, and I will listen to you. You will seek me and find me when you seek me with all your heart.
Jeremiah 29:12-13 NIV

God not only gives us answers to our prayers, but with every answer gives us something of Himself.

Prayer is a rising up and a drawing near to God in mind, and in heart, and in spirit.

Draw near to God
and He will draw
near to you.
James 4:8 NASB

Whatever you did for one of the least of these brothers of mine, you did for me.
Matthew 25:40
NIV

He does good to himself who does good to his friend.

Keep company with good men and good men you will imitate.

Iron sharpeneth iron; so a man sharpeneth the countenance of his friend.
Proverbs 27:17

*If we are faithless,
He will remain
faithful, for
he cannot dis-
own himself.*
2 Timothy 2:13
NIV

Decisions can take you out of God's will but never out of His reach.

If you have stumbled, O seeker of God, do not just lie there fretting and bemoaning your weakness! Patiently pray: "Lord, I acknowledge that every moment I would be stumbling if you were not upholding me." And then get up! Leap! Walk! Go on your way! *Run with resolution the race* in which you are entered.

Let us also lay aside every encumbrance, and the sin which so easily entangles us, and let us run with endurance the race that is set before us, fixing our eyes on Jesus, the author and perfecter of faith.
Hebrews 12:1-2
NASB

But now hath God set the members every one of them in the body, as it hath pleased him.
1 Corinthians 12:18

Be content in the calling God has placed you.

The secret of contentment is the realization that life is a gift, not a right.

But godliness with contentment is great gain. For we brought nothing into this world, and it is certain we can carry nothing out.
1 Timothy 6:6-7

For if ye forgive men their trespasses, your heavenly Father will also forgive you: But if ye forgive not men their trespasses, neither will your Father forgive your trespasses.
Matthew 6:14-15

To forgive is to set a prisoner free and discover the prisoner was *you.*

He who forgives first, wins.

...forgiving each other, just as in Christ God forgave you.
Ephesians 4:32
NIV

Ye have not,
because ye
ask not.
James 4:2

Some people think God does not like to be troubled with our constant coming and asking. The only way to trouble God is not to come at all.

God's giving is inseparably connected with our asking.

You do not have,
because you
do not ask.
James 4:2 NRSV

The love toward our neighbors must be like the pure and chaste love between bride and bride-groom, where all faults are connived at [overlooked] and borne with, and only the virtues regarded.

Now that you have purified yourselves by obeying the truth so that you have sincere love for your brothers, love one another deeply, from the heart.
1 Peter 1:22 NIV

Who seeks a faultless friend remains friendless.

Bear one another's burdens, and so fulfil the law of Christ.
Galatians 6:2 RSV

For the grace of God that brings salvation has appeared to all men. It teaches us to say "No" to ungodliness and worldly passions, and to live self-controlled, upright and godly lives in this present age.
Titus 2:11-12 NIV

I scarce thought it possible for a man to retain the Christian spirit amidst the noise and bustle of the world. *God* taught me better by my own experience.

God has also, through the intercession of His Son, given us His Holy Spirit to renew us both in knowledge and also in His moral image. This being done, we know that *all things work together for our good.*

And we know that in all things God works for the good of those who love him, who have been called according to his purpose.
Romans 8:28 NIV

I have chosen the way of truth: thy judgments have I laid before me. I have stuck unto thy testimonies: O Lord, put me not to shame.

Psalm 119:30-31

The best law for Bible study is the law of perseverance. The psalmist says, "I have stuck unto thy testimonies"...Some people are like express trains; they skim along so quickly that they see nothing.

Blessed is he who delights in [the Word of God] and gladly sees this light, for it loves to shine. But moles and bats, that is, the people of the world, do not like it.

I delight in your commands because I love them.
Psalm 119:47 NIV

After this manner therefore pray ye . . . Thy kingdom come. Thy will be done in earth, as it is in heaven.
Matthew 6:9-10

Don't ask God for what you think is good; ask Him for what He thinks is good for you.

Possessions are not given that we may rely on them and glory in them but that we may use and enjoy them and share them with others …Our possessions should be in our hands, not in our hearts.

Charge them that are rich in this world, that they be not high-minded, nor trust in uncertain riches, but in the living God, who giveth us richly all things to enjoy.
1 Timothy 6:17

Evening, and morning, and at noon, will I pray, and cry aloud: and he shall hear my voice.
Psalm 55:17

No day is well spent without communication with God.

True prayer is a way of life, not just in case of emergency.

And pray in the Spirit on all occasions with all kinds of prayers and requests.
Ephesians 6:18
NIV

Be filled with the Spirit.
Ephesians 5:18

God commands us to be filled with the Spirit; and if we aren't filled, it's because we're living beneath our privileges.

The Holy Spirit gives us the inherent ability (power) to *be* witnesses of God's great love.

But you shall receive power when the Holy Spirit has come upon you; and you shall be witnesses to Me in Jerusalem, and in all Judea and Samaria, and to the end of the earth.
Acts 1:8 NKJV

Casting down imaginations, and every high thing that exalteth itself against the knowledge of God, and bringing into captivity every thought to the obedience of Christ.
2 Corinthians 10:5

One old divine says, "You are not to blame for the birds that fly over your head, but if you allow them to come down and make a nest in your hair, then you are to blame." And so with these evil thoughts that come flashing into our minds; we have to fight them.

Being tempted to sin is not a sin. Allowing the thought to stick around is.

No temptation has overtaken you except such as is common to man; but God is faithful, who will not allow you to be tempted beyond what you are able, but with the temptation will also make the way of escape, that you may be able to bear it.

1 Corinthians 10:13 NKJV

The fear of the Lord is the beginning of knowledge: but fools despise wisdom and instruction.
Proverbs 1:7

Being afraid of God is different from fearing God. The fear of God is a fruit of love, but being afraid of Him is the seed of hatred.

To fear God means to show reverence: awe, honor, and respect. It has nothing to do with being afraid.

There is no fear
in love; but
perfect love
casts out fear,
because fear
involves torment.
1 John 4:18 NKJV

A man's pride brings him low, but a man of lowly spirit gains honor.
Proverbs 29:23
NIV

It is possible to be too big for God to use you but never too small for God to use you.

God has a history of using the insignificant to accomplish the impossible.

And Jesus looking upon them saith, With men it is impossible, but not with God: for with God all things are possible.
Mark 10:27

*Cast your cares
on the Lord
and he will
sustain you.*
Psalm 55:22 NIV

It is such a comfort to drop the tangles of life into God's hands and leave them there.

Sometimes the Lord calms the storm; sometimes He lets the storm rage and calms His child.

And the peace of God, which transcends all understanding, will guard your hearts and your minds in Christ Jesus.
Philippians 4:7
NIV

A merry heart doeth good like a medicine.
Proverbs 17:22

Laughter is a tranquilizer with no side effects.

Laughter is the brush that sweeps away the cobwebs of the heart.

A happy heart is
good medicine
and a cheerful
mind works
healing, but a
broken spirit
dries up
the bones.
Proverbs 17:22
AMP

All have sinned and fall short of the glory of God, and are justified freely by his grace through the redemption that came by Christ Jesus.
Romans 3:23-24
NIV

Justification means that there isn't a charge against you. Your sins are completely wiped out; God says He puts them out of His memory.

He who is justified performs good works; for this is the meaning of Scripture: Justification precedes good works, and works are performed by those who are justified.

For we are his workmanship, created in Christ Jesus unto good works, which God hath before ordained that we should walk in them.
Ephesians 2:10

For a just man falleth seven times, and riseth up again.
Proverbs 24:16

Falling down doesn't make you a failure, but staying down does.

If you're heading in the wrong direction, God allows U-turns.

If you repent, I will restore you that you may serve me.
Jeremiah 15:19
NIV

O sing unto the Lord a new song: sing unto the Lord, all the earth. Sing unto the Lord, bless his name; shew forth his salvation from day to day.
Psalm 96:1-2

Praise is the rehearsal of our eternal song. By grace we learn to sing, and in glory we continue to sing.

Holy wonder will lead you to grateful worship.

Give unto the Lord the glory due unto his name; worship the Lord in the beauty of holiness.
Psalm 29:2

Provide things honest in the sight of all men.
Romans 12:17

Honesty is the first chapter of the book of wisdom.

The discipline of desire is the background of character.

But I keep under my body, and bring it into subjection: lest that by any means, when I have preached to others, I myself should be a castaway.
1 Corinthians 9:27

A wise man's
heart guides
his mouth.
Proverbs 16:23
NIV

Be careful of your thoughts: They may become words at any moment.

The right train of thought can take you to a better station in life.

For as he thinks within himself, so he is.
Proverbs 23:7
NASB

Blessed be the Lord, who daily loadeth us with benefits, even the God of our salvation.
Psalm 68:19

God always gives His best to those who leave the choice with Him.

If one door shall be shut, God will open another; if the peas do not yield well, the beans may; if one hen leaves her eggs, another will bring all her brood; there's a bright side to all things, and a good God everywhere.

O taste and see that the Lord is good: blessed is the man that trusteth in him.
Psalm 34:8

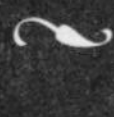

Don't be teamed with those who do not love the Lord…how can a Christian be a partner with one who doesn't believe?
2 Corinthians 6:14-15 TLB

I make it a rule of Christian duty never to go to a place where there is not room for my Master as well as myself.

Merely going to church doesn't make you a Christian any more than going to a garage makes you an automobile.

Why do you call me "Lord, Lord," and do not do what I tell you?
Luke 6:46 NRSV

If anyone serves Me, he must continue to follow me [to cleave steadfastly to Me, conform wholly to My example in living. . .]and wherever I am, there will My servant be also. If anyone serves Me, the Father will honor him.
John 12:26 AMP

To know the will of God is the greatest knowledge, to find the will of God is the greatest discovery, and to do the will of God is the greatest achievement.

The greatest use of life is to spend it for something that will outlast it.

But store up for yourselves treasures in heaven, where moth and rust do not destroy, and where thieves do not break in and steal.
Matthew 6:20
NIV

Keep watching and praying, that you may not come into temptation.
Mark 14:38 NASB

Watch out for temptation—the more you see of it the better it looks.

When you flee temptations, don't leave a forwarding address.

Now flee from youthful lusts, and pursue righteousness, faith, love and peace, with those who call on the Lord from a pure heart.

2 Timothy 2:22
NASB

By this shall all men know that ye are my disciples, if ye have love one to another.
John 13:35

It's good to be a Christian and know it, but it's better to be a Christian and show it!

A Christian must keep the faith, but not to himself.

Go ye into all
the world, and
preach the gospel
to every creature.
Mark 16:15

*A glad heart
makes a cheerful
countenance,
but by sorrow
of heart the
spirit is broken.
Proverbs 15:13*
AMP

Lay aside life-harming heaviness and entertain a cheerful disposition.

God wants us to be cheerful, and He hates sadness. For had He wanted us to be sad, He would not have given us the sun, the moon, and the various fruits of the earth. All these He gave for our good cheer.

Sing, O heavens; and be joyful, O earth; and break forth into singing, O mountains: for the Lord hath comforted his people, and will have mercy upon his afflicted.
Isaiah 49:13

Know ye that the Lord he is God; it is he that hath made us, and not we ourselves; we are his people, and the sheep of his pasture.
Psalm 100:3

The greatest act of faith is when man decides he is not God.

We cannot give God anything; for everything is already His, and all we have comes from Him. We can only give Him praise, thanks and honor.

The earth is the Lord's, and the fulness thereof; the world, and they that dwell therein.
Psalm 24:1

And let us not
grow weary in
well-doing, for
in due season we
shall reap, if we
do not lose heart.
Galatians 6:9 RSV

In trying times, don't quit trying.

God never asks about our ability or our inability —just our availability.

I heard the voice of the Lord, saying, Whom shall I send, and who will go for us? Then said I, Here am I; send me.

Isaiah 6:8

I lift up my eyes
to the hills—
where does my
help come from?
My help comes
from the Lord
. . . the Lord will
keep you from
all harm—he
will watch
over your life.
Psalm 121:1,2,7
NIV

It is impossible for that man to despair who remembers that his Helper is omnipotent.

Man's extremity is God's opportunity. When we are quite empty, the Lord will fill us.

My grace is sufficient for thee: for my strength is made perfect in weakness.
2 Corinthians 12:9

*It is written,
"Man shall not
live by bread
alone, but by
every word that
proceeds from the
mouth of God."*
Matthew 4:4 RSV

~

What is a home without a Bible? 'Tis a home where daily bread for the body is provided, but the soul is never fed.

The Christian life without prayer is like computer hardware without the software.

Call to me and I will answer you and tell you great and unsearchable things you do not know.
Jeremiah 33:3 NIV

A rope that
has three parts
wrapped together
is hard to break.
Ecclesiastes 4:12
NCV

Christian friendship is a triple-braided cord.

If I truly love another, I will obviously order my behavior in such a way as to contribute the utmost to his or her spiritual growth.

Each of us
should please
his neighbor
for his good, to
build him up.
Romans 15:2 NIV

For wisdom is
more precious
than rubies,
and nothing
you desire can
compare with her.
Proverbs 8:11 NIV

Fads come and go; wisdom and character go on forever.

Wisdom is the quality that keeps you from getting into situations where you need it.

I would have you learn this great fact: that a life of doing right is the wisest life there is. If you live that kind of life, you'll not limp or stumble as you run.

Proverbs 4:11-12 TLB

Thus you nullify the word of God by your tradition that you have handed down.
Mark 7:13 NIV

I allow no other rule, whether of faith or practice, than the Holy Scriptures.

It is dangerous to depart from Scripture...most of the controversies which have disturbed the Church have arisen from people's wanting to be wise above what is written, not contented with what God has plainly revealed there.

The Spirit clearly says that in later times some will abandon the faith and follow deceiving spirits and things taught by demons.
1 Timothy 4:1
NIV

Be devoted to one another in brotherly love. Honor one another above yourselves.
Romans 12:10 NIV

Treat your friends as you do your picture, and place them in their best light.

The best way to remember people is in prayer.

Keep praying earnestly for all Christians everywhere.
Ephesians 6:18 TLB

I beseech you therefore, brethren, by the mercies of God, that you present your bodies a living sacrifice, holy, acceptable to God, which is your reasonable service.
Romans 12:1
NKJV

My business is not to remain myself, but to make the absolute best of what God made.

Character is not made in crisis, it is only exhibited.

I have set the Lord always before me: because he is at my right hand, I shall not be moved.
Psalm 16:8

Be joyful in hope, patient in affliction, faithful in prayer.
Romans 12:12 NIV

By the grace of God which goes before us, accompanies us and follows us, continue steadily in the work of faith, in the patience of hope, and the labor of love.

He prayeth best, who loveth best.

Dear friends,
since God so
loved us, we
also ought to
love one another.
1 John 4:11 NIV

Never pay back evil for evil. Do things in such a way that everyone can see you are honest clear through.
Romans 12:17
TLB

Never does the human soul appear so strong and noble as when it forgoes revenge and dares to forgive an injury.

"I can forgive, but I cannot forget," is only another way of saying, "I will not forgive." Forgiveness ought to be like a canceled note — torn in two, and burned up, so that it never can be shown against one.

And be ye kind one to another, tenderhearted, forgiving one another, even as God for Christ's sake hath forgiven you.
Ephesians 4:32

Pray without ceasing.
1 Thessalonians 5:17

To be a Christian without prayer is no more possible than to be alive without breathing.

Living a life without prayer is like building a house without nails.

Unless the Lord builds the house, its builders labor in vain.
Psalm 127:1 NIV

Whoever wants to become great among you must be your servant, and whoever wants to be first must be slave of all.
Mark 10:43-44 NIV

Now he who...knows that we are all equal in Christ goes about his work with delight and is not concerned even though for this short time here on earth he is in more modest circumstances and in a lowlier position than another.

Love believes that it may and can do all things.

Everything is possible for him who believes.
Mark 9:23 NIV

Whatever you have learned or received or heard from me, or seen in me—put it into practice. And the God of peace will be with you.
Philippians 4:9 NIV

No one understands Scripture unless it is brought home to him, that is, unless he experiences it.

One Christian who has been tried is worth a hundred who have not been tried, for the blessing of God grows in trials. He who has experienced them can teach, comfort, and advise many in bodily and spiritual matters.

We can comfort those in any trouble with the comfort we ourselves have received from God. For just as the sufferings of Christ flow over into our lives, so also through Christ our comfort overflows.

2 Corinthians 1:4-5 NIV

The whole Bible was given to us by inspiration from God and is useful to teach us what is true and to make us realize what is wrong in our lives; it straightens us out and helps us do what is right.
2 Timothy 3:16
TLB

Here [in the Bible] is knowledge enough for me...Here then I am far from the busy ways of men. I sit down alone. Only God is here. In His presence, I open, I read His Book.

The Bible is alive, it speaks to me; it has feet, it runs after me; it has hands, it lays hold of me.

For the word of God is living and active. Sharper than any double-edged sword, it penetrates even to dividing soul and spirit, joints and marrow; it judges the thoughts and attitudes of the heart.
Hebrews 4:12 NIV

Finally, brethren, whatsoever things are true, whatsoever things are honest, whatsoever things are just...if there be any virtue, and if there be any praise, think on these things.
Philippians 4:8

A well-trained memory is one that permits you to forget everything that isn't worth remembering.

The best way to get even is to forget.

But love ye your enemies, and do good, and lend, hoping for nothing again; and your reward shall be great, and ye shall be the children of the Highest: for he is kind unto the unthankful and to the evil.

Luke 6:35

The Lord is near to all who call upon Him, to all who call upon Him sincerely and in truth.
Psalm 145:18 AMP

Prayer is conversation with God.

If you can't pray as you want to, pray as you can. God knows what you mean.

"Lord, help me!"
Matthew 15:25
NIV

But encourage
one another daily,
as long as it is
called Today.
Hebrews 3:13 NIV

We should seize every opportunity to give encouragement. Encouragement is oxygen to the soul.

A Christian should be a lamp, and not a damp. He should cheer and enlighten his brethren, and never act as a wet blanket to their zeal.

Love is always supportive, loyal, hopeful, and trusting.
1 Corinthians 13:7 CEV

Now faith is being sure of what we hope for and certain of what we do not see.
Hebrews 11:1 NIV

Faith is the 'yes' of the heart, a conviction on which one stakes one's life.

Your faith comes from Him, not from you. And everything that works faith within you comes from Him and not from you.

Do not think of yourself more highly than you ought, but rather think of yourself with sober judgment, in accordance with the measure of faith God has given you.
Romans 12:3 NIV

Giving thanks always for all things unto God and the Father in the name of our Lord Jesus Christ.
Ephesians 5:20

Life's best outlook is a prayerful uplook.

Make every matter of care a matter of prayer.

Casting all your care upon him; for he careth for you.
1 Peter 5:7

Let us not love
with words or
tongue but with
actions and
in truth.
1 John 3:18 NIV

Love is an act of will, both an intention and an action.

God's grace is the oil that fills the lamp of love.

It is God Who is all the while effectually at work in you [energizing and creating in you the power and desire], both to will and to work for His good pleasure.

Philippians 2:13 AMP

Even though you do not see him now, you...are filled with an inexpressible and glorious joy.
1 Peter 1:8 NIV

It is pleasing to God whenever you rejoice or laugh from the bottom of your heart.

Happiness is the result of circumstances, but joy endures in spite of circumstances.

In thy presence is fulness of joy; at thy right hand there are pleasures for evermore.
Psalm 16:11

How very good
and pleasant it is
when kindred live
together in unity!
Psalm 133:1 NRSV

Is any pleasure on earth as great as a circle of Christian friends by a fire?

Do not save your loving speeches
For your friends till they are dead;
Do not write them on their tombstones,
Speak them rather now instead.

Be kind to this people, and please them, and speak good words to them.
2 Chronicles 10:7

Be merciful unto me, O Lord: for I cry unto thee daily.
Psalm 86:3

I do not always bend the knee to pray; I often pray in crowded city street in some hard crisis of a busy day — prayer is my sure and comforting retreat.

There are moments when, whatever be the attitude of the body, the soul is on its knees.

My soul waits in silence for God only; from Him is my salvation.
Psalm 62:1 NASB

So Peter...walked on the water toward Jesus. But when he looked around at the high waves, he was terrified and began to sink.
Matthew 14:29-30
TLB

Obstacles are those frightful things you see when you take your eyes off the goal.

Courage is resistance to fear, mastery of fear. Not the absence of fear.

Therefore, take up the full armor of God, that you may be able to resist in the evil day, and having done everything, to stand firm. Stand firm therefore.

Ephesians 6:13-14
NASB

The eternal God is your refuge and dwelling place, and underneath are the everlasting arms.
Deuteronomy 33:27 AMP

I have been driven many times to my knees by the overwhelming conviction that I had nowhere else to go.

You are never so high as when you are on your knees.

Humble yourselves in the sight of the Lord, and he shall lift you up.
James 4:10

A man who
has friends
must himself
be friendly.
Proverbs 18:24
NKJV

The only way to have a friend is to be one.

To have a good friend is one of the highest delights of life; to be a good friend is one of the noblest and most difficult undertakings.

Greater love has no one than this, than to lay down one's life for his friends.
John 15:13 NKJV

And God is able to make all grace abound toward you; that ye, always having all sufficiency in all things, may abound to every good work.
2 Corinthians 9:8

Just when I need Him, He is my all, answering when upon Him I call; tenderly watching lest I should fall.

If we could hear Christ praying for us in the next room, we would have no fear. Yet distance makes no difference. He is praying for us.

We have an advocate with the Father, Jesus Christ the righteous.
1 John 2:1

The righteous will live by his faith.
Habakkuk 2:4
NIV

Our faith should be our steering wheel, not our spare tire.

Nothing is simpler than faith, and nothing more sublime. Faith is simple from the human side: it is a childlike trust. But it is sublime from the divine side, since it grasps the Invisible, and has power with the Omnipotent.

But Jesus looked at them and said to them, "With men this is impossible, but with God all things are possible."
Matthew 19:26
NKJV

You will keep him in perfect peace, Whose mind is stayed on You.
Isaiah 26:3 NKJV

Prayer is for the soul what nourishment is for the body.

The deepest wishes of the heart find expression in secret prayer.

For there is not a word in my tongue, but, lo, O Lord, thou knowest it altogether.
Psalm 139:4

This one thing I do, forgetting those things which are behind, and reaching forth unto those things which are before, I press toward the mark for the prize of the high calling of God in Christ Jesus.
Philippians 3:13-14

The past should be a springboard, not a hammock.

I like the dreams of the future better than the history of the past.

Remember ye not the former things, neither consider the things of old. Behold, I will do a new thing.
Isaiah 43:18-19

References

Unless otherwise indicated, all Scripture quotations are taken from the *King James Version* of the Bible.

Scripture quotations marked NIV are taken from the *Holy Bible, New International Version*® NIV®. Copyright © 1973, 1978, 1984 by International Bible Society. Used by permission of Zondervan Publishing House. All rights reserved.

Verses marked TLB are taken from *The Living Bible*, copyright ©1971. Used by permission of Tyndale House Publishers, Inc., Wheaton, Illinois 60189. All rights reserved.

Scripture quotations marked NASB are taken from the *New American Standard Bible*. Copyright © The Lockman Foundation. 1960, 1962, 1963, 1968, 1971, 1973, 1975, 1977. Used by permission.

Scripture quotations marked NKJV are taken from the *New King James Version* of the Bible. Copyright © 1979, 1980, 1982, Thomas Nelson, Inc., Publishers.

Scripture quotations marked NRSV are taken from *The New Revised Standard Version Bible*, copyright © 1989 by the Division of Christian Education of the Churches of Christ in the United States of America and is used by permission.

Scripture quotations marked RSV are taken from the *Revised Standard Version of the Bible*, copyright © 1946, *Old Testament* section copyright © 1952 by the Division of Christian Education of the Churches of Christ in the United States of America and is used by permission.

Scripture quotations marked MLB are taken from *The Modern Language Bible, The New Berkley Version in Modern English*. Copyright © 1923, 1945, 1959, 1969 by Zondervan Publishing House, Grand Rapids, Michigan.

Scripture quotations marked CEV are taken from *The Contemporary English Version*, copyright © 1995 by the American Bible Society. All rights reserved.

Verses marked NCV are scriptures quoted from *The Holy Bible, New Century Version*, copyright © 1987, 1988, 1991 by Word Publishing, Dallas, Texas 75039. Used by permission.

Acknowledgments

We acknowledge and thank the following people for the quotes used in this book: Wesley L. Duewel (6), Amy Carmichael (9), Martin Luther (10,11,44, 50,55,57,64,73,93,95,116,118,120,121,123,130,131,136,144), Dwight L. Moody (13,16,17,25,32,48,54,60,62,72), John Wesley (14,15,22,23,33,43,52,53,106, 107,112,122), Charles Malik (18), William James (19), Les Brown (24), Dr. James Dobson (26), Abraham Joshua Heschel (28), Louis Cassels (29), Billy Graham (30), C. Everett Koop (34), John Sculley (35), George Sala (36), Bear Bryant (37), Alexander Whyte (39), Erasmus (40), William Penn (47), Andrew Murray (49), Richard Exley (67), Mercelene Cox (70), Mort Walker (71), Charles Haddon Spurgeon (76,77,83,99,129,151), Thomas Jefferson (78), John Locke (79), Jim Elliot (82), John Newton (84), Billy Sunday (85), Arnold H. Glasow (86), Bacon (87), Jim Patrick (91), Oliver Wendell Holmes (94), Jeremy Taylor (98), Charles Megis (100), M. Scott Peck (103), Norman Vincent Peale (105), Jennie Jerome Churchill (108), Robert Browning (110), Hudson Taylor (111), Samuel Taylor Coleridge (113), E.H. Chapin (114), C.G. Jung (115), W.E. Sangster & Leslie Davison (117), Thomas A Kempis (119), Clement of